CELEBRATIONS AND RITUALS

everyday celebrations & rituals

CHERRYTREE BOOKS

Published in the UK by Cherrytree Books, part of the
Evans Publishing Group
2A Portman Mansions
Chiltern Street
London W1U 6NR

First published in paperback in 2007.

In the same series:
End-of-Life Rituals
Marriage Celebrations
Celebrating Prophets & Gods
Winter Celebrations

British Library Cataloguing-in-Publication Data

Matthews, Rupert
 Everyday. – (Celebrations and rituals)
 1. Rites and ceremonies – Juvenile literature 2. Manners and
customs – Juvenile literature
 I. Title II. Senker, Cath
 390

 ISBN 978 1 84234 400 2

Printed and bound in China by C&C Offset

1 2 3 4 5 6 7 8 9 10 09 08 07 06 05 04 03

McRae Books:
Publishers: Anne McRae and Marco Nardi
Series Editor: Loredana Agosta
Graphic Design: Marco Nardi
Layout: Sebastiano Ranchetti
Picture Research: Loredana Agosta
Cutouts: Filippo delle Monache, Alman Graphic Design
Text: Rupert Matthews, Cath Senker

Illustrations: Studio Stalio (Alessandro Cantucci, Fabiano Fabbrucci,
Andrea Morandi, Ivan Stalio), Paula Holguin, MM Illustrazioni
(Manuela Cappon), Alessandro Menchi, Antonella Pastorelli, Paola
Ravaglia

Colour Separations: Litocolor, Florence (Italy)

Copyright © 2003, McRae Books Srl

Borgo Santa Croce 8—Florence, Italy.
info@mcraebooks.com

Acknowledgements
The Publishers would like to thank the following photographers
and picture libraries for the photos used in this book.
t=top; tl=top left; tc=top centre; tr=top right; c=centre; cl=centre
left; cr=centre right; b= bottom; bl=bottom left; bc=bottom
centre; br=bottom right
A.S.A.P Picture Library: 25br; Bernadette Heath: 34tr; Marco Lanza:
31br, 40tr; Lonely Planet Images: Gregory Adams cover, Mark
Daffey 11tr, Chris Beall 12cl, Graham Taylor 13tr, Paul Beinssen
16cr, Gregory Adams 16bl, Greg Elms 19tr, Antony Giblin 20bl,
Richard l'Anson 21cr, Martin Hughes 21bl, Anders Blomquist 23tr,
Anthony Pidgeon 24bl, Martin Moss 29br, Simon Bracken 30bl,
Alison Wright 36bl, David Peevers 37br, Ariadne Van Zandbergen
39bc, Frances Linzee Gordon 41cl, Casey Mahaney 42c; The Image
Works: 10c, 12bl, 14br, 15tr, 17tl, 18cl, 19cl, 22tr, 22b, 26bl, 27tl, 30cl,
31tr, 32br, 33tl, 33br, 39tr, 40bl, 41br, 42b

everyday celebrations & rituals

CHERRYTREE BOOKS

Table of Contents

Everyday Rituals

Introduction

In ancient Rome, people worshipped the lares each morning with prayers and offerings. Lares were spirits who protected the home.

Throughout the world special rituals enrich everyday life. Deeply rooted in culture, tradition and religion, these rituals give special meaning or significance to eating, greeting others, dressing, religious worship, inviting guests, housekeeping and hygiene (keeping oneself clean). In addition, everyday rituals are a way for people to express their cultural identity. Religion plays an important role in everyday life for worshippers all over the world. Religious devotion, such as praying and making offerings to God, the gods or spirits, are part of the daily routine for many. Some religions also have rules about eating, dressing and conducting relations with others. In addition to religion, customs and traditions dictate formal rules of behaviour called etiquette.

During the traditional Japanese tea ceremony special instruments are used to prepare tea for honoured guests.

This traditional Tibetan tongue gesture is a way of showing respect.

When worshippers pray in a mosque, they face an arched niche called a mihrab to ensure they are facing Mecca, Islam's holiest city. Prayer is an important part of daily life for Muslims.

GREETINGS AROUND THE WORLD

BOLIVIA

An Aymara woman says hello to friends by tipping her bowler hat.

JAPAN

Japanese bow from the waist.

NEW ZEALAND

Maori greet each other with the traditional hongi by pressing their noses together.

THAILAND

Thais greet one another by clasping their hands together at the chest and bowing slightly.

ZAMBIA

Friends shake their right hand with their left hand held below the right elbow.

Rituals of the Past

In ancient times, some rituals were grand occasions involving thousands of people. Others were small, private affairs for families or individuals. Some combined both aspects, with a few people performing a ritual on behalf of a society. Modern scholars know about some of these rituals through the writings of people who lived in ancient times and from archaeological findings. However, some ancient rituals remain difficult to understand.

In the Temple of Vesta in Rome, a sacred fire always burned as a symbol of the well-being of the Roman state.

Ancient Celebrations

Health, Well-Being and Survival

In ancient times, the purpose of many rituals was to ensure that systems of the natural world and daily life continued smoothly, without famine or disease. In ancient America, both the Maya (about A.D. 250–900) and the Aztecs (about A.D. 1200–1521) played a special ball game to honour the gods of the sun and crops. They believed the game would ensure that the gods would continue to provide food for their people. Sometimes the losing team was sacrificed to the gods in a bloody ritual. In ancient Rome (753 B.C.–A.D. 476), the hearth (fireplace floor) was sacred to the goddess Vesta. To honour Vesta, Romans kept a sacred fire burning continuously in her temple in Rome. Priestesses called Vestal Virgins never married and kept the fire lit. If they failed, they were whipped.

Vestal Virgins tend the sacred fire in ancient Rome.

Ancient Aztec warriors play a ball game that formed part of religious worship in Central America.

Mixtecs from ancient Mexico (A.D. 900-1520) share a foaming cup of chocolate to celebrate a marriage in this drawing from the 1300s.

Food Preparation and Mealtimes

Many rituals surrounded food and drink. The ancient Greeks believed wine was sacred to the god Dionysus and held wild dances in his honour during the wine harvest. In ancient Egypt, ploughing the soil was so important that no one was allowed to begin farming until the pharaoh (the king) performed a ritual breaking of the soil near a temple. In ancient America, beverages made from the cacao bean, whose seeds are used to make chocolate, were used in religious rituals and to celebrate such important events as marriages and births.

Omens, Superstitions and Predictions

People have long sought a method of predicting the future. The ancient Greeks asked questions of prophets or prophetesses, called oracles, who were believed to be in direct communication with the gods. The most famous was the Oracle at Delphi, who spoke for the sun god, Apollo. This prophetess sat on a special stool and answered questions put to her. Sometimes the answers were a clear "yes" or "no", but often they were complex and mysterious. The Romans consulted a set of written predictions called the *Sibylline* in times of danger. During festival processions in ancient Egypt, priests carried an image of the goddess Hathor. Simple yes or no questions were asked, and the answers were determined by the way in which the image moved.

An ancient Greek consults the Oracle of Delphi, who is seated on a three-legged stool.

Medieval Christian nuns sit in church reading the Bible.

Religious Devotion

In many societies, some people have carried out religious duties on behalf of everyone else. In ancient Egypt, hundreds of men served in the temples to carry out complex religious ceremonies. These men had to shave their bodies completely, cutting off even their eyelashes. In medieval Europe, many men and women lived in monasteries or convents, where they devoted themselves full time to the worship of God and to learning. In Tibet, some monasteries housed thousands of monks who performed Lamaist rituals.

Etiquette, Greetings and Forms of Address

Rituals used to greet others are among the most important of all rituals. If these are ignored, the person being greeted may be offended or even become hostile. Today, we often shake hands to show we are friendly. In ancient China, people meeting a government official had to kow-tow—that is, kneel and touch the forehead to the ground. In 1528, an Italian writer named Baldassare Castiglione (1478-1529) wrote a book on court etiquette that influenced social behaviour in Spain, France, England and Italy for many years.

Baldassare Castiglione set the standards for proper behaviour among ladies and gentleman of the 1500s. He believed a gentleman had to be physically fit, knowledgeable about the arts and an eloquent speaker.

Daily Life in China

A pair of chopsticks and an empty bowl wait for each diner at a Chinese meal.

Many of China's everyday rituals and customs are thousands of years old. Some are based on religion, some on philosophy and some on Chinese culture. In traditional Chinese society, rituals are extremely important and are carried out very carefully. Knowledge of these rituals is passed on from parents to children so that each new generation learns the customs of its ancestors.

This lacquer tea set may have belonged to an upper-class family. Preparing tea is an elaborate process designed to show honour to a guest.

The Far East

A mother teaches her child how to use chopsticks to pick up food politely.

THE FAR EAST

The Far East is the eastern-most part of Asia. Asia extends from Africa and Europe in the west to the Pacific Ocean in the east. The northernmost part of the continent is in the Arctic. In the south, Asia ends in the tropics near the equator. Traditionally, the term Far East has referred to China, Japan, North Korea, South Korea, Taiwan and eastern Siberia in Russia. Southeast Asia includes Borneo, Brunei, Cambodia, East Timor, Indonesia, Laos, Malaysia, Myanmar, the Philippines, Singapore, Thailand and Vietnam.

Food Preparation and Mealtimes

Food plays an important role in Chinese society. When friends meet, they politely ask, "Have you eaten well today"? At the dinner table, each diner has a bowl, and all the dishes of food are placed in the centre of the table. The guest of honour or head of the household helps himself or herself first. If fish is served, the dish is placed so that the head is pointing toward the guest of honour or head of the household. Diners are expected to finish eating anything they have placed in their bowl, because leftover food is a serious insult to the cook. It is also considered insulting to eat with the bowl on the table; it should be picked up and held close to the mouth. In addition, polite Chinese slurp their soup. At the end of the meal, no one may leave the table before the chief guest.

Etiquette, Greetings and Forms of Address

The Chinese philosopher Kong Qiu, also known as Confucius, founded a philosophy that emphasises correct behaviour and living in harmony. According to Confucianism, older or more senior members of society should be respected, and superiors should treat inferiors with tact and grace. Confucius taught that an important way of achieving this was by following proper greeting rituals that recognise the rank of the person being met.

The Chinese philosopher Kong Qiu, also known as Confucius, lived from about 551 B.C. to about 479 B.C. A member of a noble family, he worked as a government official.

A woman uses a fan as she completes a t'ai chi exercise to prepare her body for the day's activities.

Health, Well-Being and Survival

The Chinese religion of Taoism teaches that people, animals, the world and the gods are part of the Tao (Way). Tao is a current of negative and positive forces known as yin and yang. Taoists believe that yin and yang must remain in perfect balance to ensure that people remain healthy and prosperous. To do this, Taoists practise yoga, t'ai chi, or breathing exercises. They also meditate to gain understanding of the Tao. Before any important event, Taoist priests carry out rituals to ensure that yin and yang are in balance.

Omens, Superstitions and Predictions

At least 3,000 years ago, the Chinese began trying to divine the future by means of the *I Ching* (*Book of Changes*). In response to a question, a priest throws a group of sticks on the ground. He then inspects the way they cross one another or lie separately to decide which of 64 patterns they most closely resemble. Finally, he consults the *Book of Changes* to see what this pattern means in relation to the question.

Chinese men perform an I Ching ceremony. After the sticks are thrown down, a prediction is made. Incense is burned to attract the attention of the gods.

Asia's Minorities

Asia is a vast continent with many different ethnic and national groups. Some nations are made up of a single or dominant group of people, while other nations or regions may contain one main (majority) group and several smaller (minority) groups. Minority groups may be integrated in the population of a country, or they may live largely by themselves in a particular region. In some areas, minorities live much as they have for centuries. In others, the cultures and festivals of minority groups are changing as the people adapt to modern lifestyles.

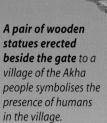

A woven basket from the Lahu people is used to store grain and other foods.

A pair of wooden statues erected beside the gate to a village of the Akha people symbolises the presence of humans in the village.

A bowl of tsampa is enjoyed by a Tibetan boy in Tingri.

Health, Well-Being and Survival

The Akha people of northern Thailand maintain a culture centred on their villages. They believe that outside the village live not only leopards, snakes and other dangerous animals, but also evil demons and wild spirits of the forest. To protect the villagers from these bad influences, the Akha erect a sacred gate across each path into the village. The gate consists of two upright wooden poles topped by a third. When people enter or leave the village, they must pass through this gate to ensure they are free of spirits. Beside each gate stand two wooden statues of a man and a woman, whose presence indicates that the village is a dwelling place of human beings, not spirits. Although new gates and statues are erected each year, the old ones are not removed but are simply left to rot.

A woman of the Jingpo people of southern China wears a festive dress. The Jingpo carry bamboo tubes filled with wine.

Guests and Hospitality

Among many of the minority groups of Asia, the arrival of a guest is an occasion for many rituals. These are aimed at making the guest feel welcome and honoured. In Tibet, a visitor is welcomed to a house with a bowl of hot tea, in which floats butter made from yak's milk. If the visitor is particularly welcome, he or she may receive a dish of tsampa, a type of biscuit made by mixing roasted barley flour with butter, sugar and tea. The Jingpo people of southern China store wine in wide bamboo tubes. A Jingpo woman welcomes a visitor with a cup of wine. The Jingpo carry small bamboo tubes of wine with them and offer a drink to friends they meet.

BUILDING A GER

Some Mongols, Buryats and other minority peoples of central Asia move often in order to find fresh pasture for their large herds of horses, cattle or sheep. Some of these peoples live in a traditional home called a ger or yurt. These tentlike structures consist of a wooden frame covered with a double layer of felt. Rugs and blankets line the interior. The ger is easy to erect or take down and can be loaded onto two or three pack horses for transport. Wherever it is erected, the ger must face south, a custom that may have developed because of the cold north winds that sweep across central Asia. Traditionally, a guest is seated to the right of the ger's entrance. Each year, the family dedicates a week to repairing its ger and to adding embroidered illustrations of events of the previous year or of famous events in the family's history.

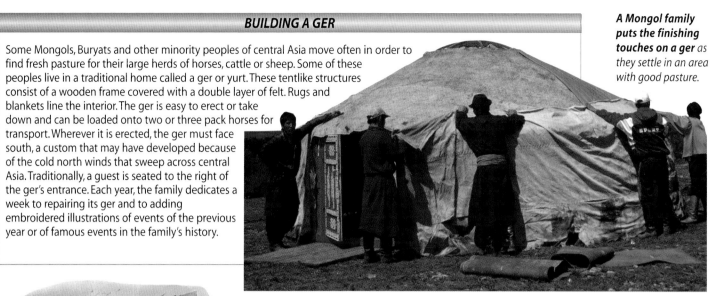

A Mongol family puts the finishing touches on a ger as they settle in an area with good pasture.

Some houses of the Yi people are decorated with painted handprints, which are believed to ward off evil spirits.

A wooden carving serves as an offering inside a Lahu temple.

At Home

Many minority groups in Asia have special rituals and beliefs about their homes. The Lisu of northern Thailand, for instance, refuse to build their houses close to one another. As a result, their villages may cover large areas. The Lisu also will not build a house within sight of running water, because they believe streams and rivers are the homes of powerful spirits. The Yi people of southwestern China erect a hollow bamboo pole outside their houses. When a family wishes to celebrate, they fill the pole with wine and invite all passers-by to have a drink.

Religious Devotion

Although some of the ethnic minorities of Asia have adopted Buddhism, Islam or Taoism as their religion, others follow religions that are unique to their group. The Lisu, for instance, believe that each village has a powerful guardian god. One man in each village is chosen to be the priest. He cares for the guardian shrine and acts as a go-between for the villagers with the spirit. The Lahu build a temple in the centre of each village to Guisha, their chief god. Every full moon, the villagers gather at the temple for a feast. Every family brings food.

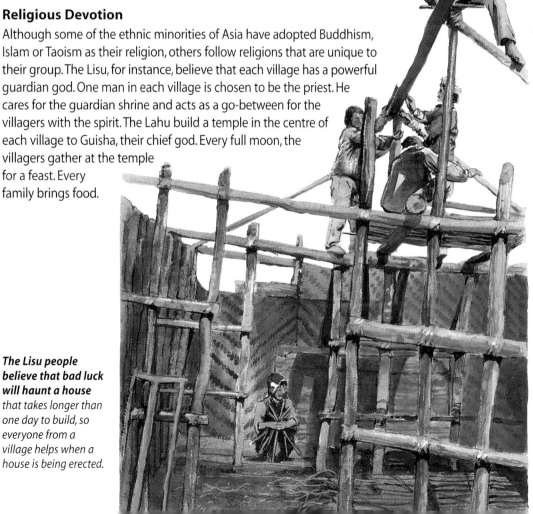

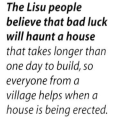

The Lisu people believe that bad luck will haunt a house that takes longer than one day to build, so everyone from a village helps when a house is being erected.

Rituals in Japan

A delicate Japanese water container called a mizusashi is used during the tea ceremony.

People have lived on the islands of Japan for more than 30,000 years. Over the centuries, the Japanese developed a unique and dynamic culture strongly influenced by the religions of Buddhism and Shinto. From the mid-1600s to the mid-1800s, Japan banned nearly all foreigners from their country, insulating their customs and rituals from outside contact. Although customs from other countries are practised in modern Japan, native Japanese traditions remain strong.

An Indian prince named Bodhidharma taught the principles of Zen in China in the A.D. 500s.

ZEN BUDDHISM

Although relatively few Japanese follow a form of Buddhism known as Zen, Zen's influence on Japanese culture is profound. Buddhism was founded in India, but Zen Buddhism was developed in China and reached Japan in the A.D. 1100s. Zen teaches that the enlightenment and mental peace sought by Buddhists can be achieved by meditating properly. The quiet contemplation of beautiful things that Zen encourages has become a major feature of Japanese life and art.

A Zen manuscript from the 1300s displays the careful production of beautiful pictures and script typical of Zen work.

JAPANESE GARDENS tend to be small. The most famous are Zen rock gardens in which no plants grow. Instead, rocks, stones and sand of different colours and textures are combined to form a three-dimensional picture.

The tea ceremony dates back over 800 years. Guests sit in a special room while the hostess makes tea using special utensils in a complex ceremony. Conversation is allowed after the tea has been drunk.

Food Preparation and Mealtimes

Japanese breakfast and lunch are generally light meals, but dinner is a bigger event. Even at private family meals, the dinner follows three equally important traditional guides: taste, appearance and dinnerware and utensils. For example, the choice of dinnerware should complement the taste and appearance of the food served on it. Each dish of food is carefully arranged before being served. The Japanese consider it impolite to serve oneself a drink, so each diner serves the person next to him or her.

Etiquette, Greetings and Forms of Address

The traditional form of greeting in Japan is a bow. Usually a younger person bows more deeply than an older person, to show respect for age, unless the younger person is of a higher status in some way. In recent years, it has become increasingly important to present a card with one's name, address and occupation when meeting a person for the first time. The cards are exchanged while bowing, and it is considered polite to read a card carefully before putting it in one's pocket. The Japanese believe it is very rude to ask a direct question or to contradict someone. They prefer to talk about a problem using indirect language.

Japanese children greet their grandparents by kneeling and bowing.

Dress and Hygiene

Traditional Japanese costumes are usually worn only on special occasions. However, some women wear a simple form of the traditional kimono around the house. A kimono is a voluminous gown of silk with loose sleeves. The kimono is gathered at the waist by a colourful sash. In Japan, people often bathe together, either with family at home or with friends at a public bath. Everyday hygiene activities, such as blowing the nose or coughing, are considered very rude. People are expected to do these in private.

Japanese family members often bathe together at home. Large baths that can accommodate parents and children are common in Japanese homes.

A shoe rack sits beside the door of every Japanese home, temple and bathhouse. There, visitors leave their shoes and put on indoor slippers.

At Home

The Japanese consider feet to be unclean parts of the body. They believe it is rude to sit with the soles of the feet facing anyone. For this reason, Japanese usually kneel with their feet tucked under their body. When entering a house, visitors are expected to remove their shoes and put on a pair of slippers provided by the host. In addition to showing respect for the homeowner, changing shoes helps keep the floors clean. This is important as the Japanese sit on the floor rather than on chairs. Some people even provide separate slippers for guests entering the bathroom, which is considered a room of special cleanliness.

Customs in Southeast Asia

Southeast Asia, which covers the large number of islands and peninsulas of Asia south of China and east of India, embraces a wide variety of cultures and nations. In the upland forests, isolated groups and people live by subsistence farming (producing crops for a farmer and his or her family only) and have little contact with the outside world. On the coastal plains lie large farms where rice, sugar and rubber are grown for sale abroad. In some areas, Islam is the main religion. Buddhism dominates other areas, while some groups have retained other traditional religions and beliefs. This mosaic of influences has created cultures with an abundance of rituals.

This cili from Bali is a Hindu offering made of palm leaves. It represents the god for whom it was made.

Worshippers at a temple in Thailand make offerings to the gods. People living in the lowlands of Thailand practise Buddhism.

THE KINGS OF THAILAND were once considered to be demigods with supernatural powers. To emphasise the difference between themselves and ordinary people, the royals had their own language, which was used only in the royal court.

A girl on the Indonesian island of Bali carries a basket of offerings to one of the thousands of temples on the island.

Religious Devotion

Although Indonesia is primarily Islamic, some other religions are also practised there. Hindu customs, which predate Islam in the area, have mingled with local traditions of ancestral worship. Many Indonesians make daily offerings to the gods. Each morning, the mother of a family offers a few grains of rice or salt at the household shrine as a gift to the ancestors or family spirits. In the afternoon, the rice is replaced with flowers. More elaborate offerings are made at important ceremonies. At weddings, banana leaves are cut and sewn into a variety of shapes and designs or decorated with bananas. At funerals, the bananas are replaced by coconuts and gifts made from coconut leaves. Although many hours of hard work may go into the preparation of these offerings, they are not kept. Once a ceremony is over and the gods or spirits have accepted a gift, the object is destroyed. All devotions are accompanied by the sounding of a percussion instrument called a gong. It is struck to different rhythms depending on the ceremony being performed.

A woman in the Philippines greets a respected older member of the family by touching her forehead to the older woman's hand.

Etiquette, Greetings and Forms of Address

Throughout Southeast Asia, the act of meeting and greeting others is accompanied by simple but rigidly defined rituals that indicate the relationship between the two people and the status of each in society. It is considered essential to avoid giving offence or causing embarrassment, so the precise form of greeting, gesture and words said are repeated. In Thailand, formal greetings and partings are accompanied by flowers arranged in a garland. Small garlands, in the form of bracelets, may be given as a parting gift or simply as a way of paying respect to an older or more important person.

A malai (garland) from Thailand consists of two strands of flowers strung together and linked by a coloured ribbon.

Health, Well-Being and Survival

In Indonesia, many rituals and celebrations are accompanied by a shadow puppet play called Wayang Kulit. A sheet is hung in front of a bright light. The puppeteer uses flat puppets to cast shadows on the sheet and to perform shows based on epic tales from Indian and Indonesian history and legend. Often, the puppeteer includes jokes or comments about current politics, about people present at the show or about recent events in the news. The shows usually include musicians as well as the puppeteer. On large formal occasions, as many as 25 people and 100 puppets may be involved. Different plays are staged for different purposes. For instance, the Ruwatan play is performed to chase away bad luck.

A flat puppet used in the Ruwatan ritual chases away bad luck. The puppet is controlled by thin sticks attached to its head and hands.

The Minangkabau people traditionally build their houses with roofs shaped like upswept buffalo horns, which are considered a sign of strength and courage.

At Home

The mountain peoples of Southeast Asia consider the design and layout of their houses important to their way of life. Among the Minangkabau of Sumatra in western Indonesia, for instance, an entire family, except the adult male children, lives in one large house. Visitors to the house are welcomed in the kitchen, where the old women sleep, and are rarely admitted to the other rooms unless they are related to the family. Children of the family sleep in the central hall of the house and move to bedrooms when they marry.

Rituals in India

Because most Indians are Hindus, many Indian rituals come from Hindu traditions. Although Indian rituals may vary by region, certain rituals are common throughout this vast land. For example, a gracious gesture called namaste is the traditional Hindu greeting. The home is considered a sacred place. Throughout India, many people remove their shoes before entering a house as a mark of respect. Daily puja (worship) takes place in the home at the family shrine. Larger homes may have a special shrine room. In smaller homes, part of a room is set aside for puja.

Melons painted with traditional devil faces are placed in homes in Tamil Nadu, India, to ward off evil spirits.

Two Indian women greet each other with the traditional namaste ritual.

South and Central Asia

Etiquette, Greetings and Forms of Address

A person using the namaste greeting places the two palms together in front of the chest and bows his or her head while saying "namaste". Indians use this greeting with younger people, older people, friends and strangers. They also say it when parting. Critically, it means "Not me, they" which is a profession of faith to the gods. When people meet elders on special occasions, they touch the elders' feet as a sign of respect. The elder person places his or her hand on the younger person's head in blessing.

At Home

The Indian home is considered a sacred place, with the kitchen the heart of the family. Many people live in extended families, with parents, grandparents and even aunts and uncles all under the same roof. Every home has a shrine with murtis (images) of gods and goddesses. Devout Hindus worship at the shrine every morning and evening. Because the home is a holy place, the family and guests usually remove their shoes, which are seen as unclean, before entering.

SOUTH AND CENTRAL ASIA

South and Central Asia are areas of distinct cultures and peoples. These regions form an area at the base of Asia. Asia extends from Africa and Europe in the west to the Pacific Ocean in the east. The northernmost part of the continent is in the Arctic. In the south, Asia ends in the tropics near the equator. South Asia is made up of Afghanistan, Armenia, Bangladesh, Bhutan, India, the Maldives, Nepal, Pakistan, Sri Lanka, the Tibetan plateau in southwest China and parts of the countries of Azerbaijan and Georgia. Much of India, the largest country in south Asia, forms a peninsula that extends southward into the Indian Ocean. Central Asia includes the countries of Kazakhstan, Kyrgyzstan, Tajikistan, Turkmenistan, Uzbekistan and the West Siberian Plain.

A chappal is the most common shoe in India. It is worn by people of all ages. The traditional style consists of a band across the middle of the foot and a toe strap.

Religious Devotion

Hindus worship before murtis that are placed in shrines. The murtis represent different aspects of Brahman, believed by Hindus to be the divine force that sustains the universe. People bathe before morning worship and before attending puja at the temple so that they appear pure before Brahman. To begin puja, worshippers ring a bell to gain the attention of the god or goddess. Incense sticks are lit. Then they pray and make offerings, such as fruit, rice and sweets to a murti. Next, lamps are lit, and worshippers make a circle of light around the image. Finally, the food offerings are eaten. They are seen as a gift and blessing.

Indian women, above, *perform puja by the River Ganges, which is sacred to Hindus.*

A bowl of fruit is a common offering to a murti. Once the food has been offered, it is known as prasada (blessed food).

ACCORDING TO INDIAN TRADITION, SALT BRINGS GOOD LUCK because it mixes well with many kinds of food. Many people make salt the first thing they buy in the new year to bring good luck to their home. Also, many folk traditions are connected to salt. For example, waving salt mixed with mustard seeds and chilies over the head of a child is believed to ward off evil spirits.

Almost all Indians eat with the right hand, as are these schoolchildren eating breakfast. Traditionally, the left hand is seen as impure and is used only for lifting a cup or glass at mealtimes.

Food Preparation and Mealtimes

Religion strongly influences the way Indians eat. Hindus do not eat beef because the cow is sacred to them. Muslims do not eat meat from the pig, which is considered unclean. Many Indians, especially in the south, are vegetarian. They respect all life and therefore will not eat animals.

Health, Well-Being and Survival

The word 'yoga' means 'spiritual path.' It is the name for an ancient school of Hindu thought and practice. Yoga involves training the mind and body through meditation, special ways of breathing and different body positions, called postures. It helps people to concentrate their mind and bring their body under control. Those who practise it also aim to follow a moral code. They should not lie, steal, cheat or harm living things.

This woman is in a cross-legged sitting position known as the Lotus pose. It is one of the meditative positions of yoga.

Jain Rituals

Ambika was reborn as a Jain goddess after leaping into a well to escape her husband, who was angry with her for giving money to a monk.

About 4 million Jains live around the world, though most live in India. They do not believe in a god. Instead, they follow the teachings of 24 Jain spiritual leaders who, they believe, have attained enlightenment (heightened awareness) since the beginning of the world. Jains try to live with as few possessions as possible. They believe that true happiness comes from inside, not from material objects. Jains are taught to meditate daily and give generously to charity.

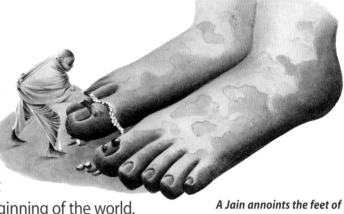

A Jain annoints the feet of a statue of Lord Bahubali, one of the enlightened beings revered by Jains.

NOT HARMING ANY LIVING THING IS A FUNDAMENTAL BELIEF OF JAINISM. Monks use a broom to sweep away any living creatures in their path so they do not accidentally step on them and kill them. Devout Jains wear a mask so that they do not accidentally inhale or swallow any insects.

Religious Devotion

Jain monks and nuns take five vows that they believe will bring them to enlightenment. The five vows are ahimsa, not to harm any living thing; satya, to speak the truth; asteya, not to steal; brahmacharya, not to have sex and aparigraha, to give up worldly things. Other Jains follow most of these principles, but they can marry and possess some material things. Jains are strict vegetarians because they do not want to harm animals.

Monks from the Shvetamabara sect, one of the two main sects of Jainism, wear simple robes. Monks from the Digambara sect wear only loincloths, or are naked.

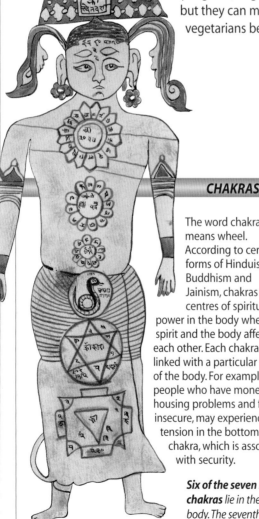

CHAKRAS

The word chakra means wheel. According to certain forms of Hinduism, Buddhism and Jainism, chakras are centres of spiritual power in the body where the spirit and the body affect each other. Each chakra is linked with a particular part of the body. For example, people who have money or housing problems and feel insecure, may experience tension in the bottom chakra, which is associated with security.

Six of the seven main chakras lie in the body. The seventh sits above the head.

ACCORDING TO JAIN TRADITION, Vardhamana Mahavira, who founded the Jain faith in the 500s B.C., did not wear any clothes after he became a monk. Mahavira's nakedness symbolised his non-attachment to worldly things.

Sikh Customs

The Sikhs, the followers of Sikhism, live mainly in Punjab, a state in northwestern India. Sikhs, who are very devout, try to direct each day's activities to God. They place a high value on family and the community. All Sikhs give seva (service to their community) by donating money to charity and helping others. The Sikh holy book is the *Guru Granth Sahib (Book of God)*, which is read during worship and at festivals. The gurdwara (temple) is the focal point for Sikh religious life. There, Sikhs gather to pray and to share langar, a communal meal.

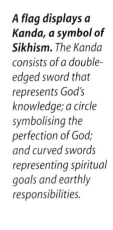

A flag displays a Kanda, a symbol of Sikhism. The Kanda consists of a double-edged sword that represents God's knowledge; a circle symbolising the perfection of God; and curved swords representing spiritual goals and earthly responsibilities.

Food Preparation and Mealtimes

After worship, Sikhs gather in the gurdwara dining room to share langar. Visitors are also welcome to enjoy the meal. This meal reflects the Sikh ideal of providing service to others, whatever their religion or background. Everyone sits together, usually on the ground, to show that all people are equal. Both men and women take turns preparing and serving langar, which is vegetarian.

Sikhs work hard to prepare langar for the 30,000 pilgrims who visit the Golden Temple daily.

In Amritsar, India, Sikhs wash the walkway around the Golden Temple, the holiest Sikh shrine. This is done daily as an act of devotion.

Religious Devotion

Sikhs meet at the gurdwara for prayers. Upon arrival, they remove their shoes and cover their head. During the service, they listen to a reading from the *Guru Granth Sahib*, which is read by a granthi, a person who has learned to read the holy book. They also sing hymns called kirtan. The service ends with a final prayer. Then everyone receives a special sweet called karah parshad.

The sacred chauri (whisk) is waved over the Guru Granth Sahib *when it is carried or read as a mark of respect.*

Daily Life of Buddhist Monks

A Tibetan prayer wheel contains tiny paper scrolls with thousands of prayers on them. Spinning the wheel releases the prayers into the world.

In Buddhist countries, communities of monks and nuns are a familiar part of everyday life. In some countries, such as Myanmar and Thailand, young men join a monastery for part of their education. Monks wear special robes and lead very simple lives, studying, meditating and chanting. The main task of all monks and nuns is teaching the community how to follow the Buddhist way. Everything they do is part of their religious devotion. They rise early in the morning for puja and meditation. Time for study and debate follows. Cleaning and maintaining the monastery and preparing food are other important jobs. In some places, monks may farm the land, too.

Religious Devotion

Buddhists are taught five basic rules. These are not to harm living things; not to take anything that has not been freely given; to tell the truth; to keep a clear mind and to try to be kind and generous. Buddhist monks and nuns are devout people who pass on the Buddha's teachings, called the dharma, to the community. Buddhists believe that if people follow the dharma, they, too, can become Buddhas and achieve enlightenment. Enlightenment is a state of heightened awareness in which a person achieves perfect peace and blessedness.

A monk studies the Buddhist scriptures, called the **Pali Canon.** *The Pali Canon is the oldest collection of Buddhist holy writings containing the Buddha's teachings.*

A Tibetan woman spins a prayer wheel. Huge prayer wheels are found at Tibetan temples.

Buddhist monks use coloured sand to make a mandala, a ritual diagram used by Buddhists of certain traditions. These monks are wearing masks so as not to breathe in the sand. People meditate on the mandala, which represents the universe.

Food Preparation and Mealtimes

In countries where Buddhist monks and nuns live separately from the rest of the community, they rely on local people for their food. Every morning, the monks and nuns leave their monasteries with their empty bowls to beg for food. They return to share the food they have received among themselves and eat their one daily meal. People enjoy feeding the monks because helping others is central to Buddhism. In return, the monks teach people the Buddhist way of life.

Dress and Hygiene

Buddhist monks and nuns wear robes and either shave their heads or wear their hair very short. In Sri Lanka and Thailand they wear saffron-coloured robes; in Tibet, they wear maroon. Japanese monks wear black robes. Traditionally, Buddhist monks and nuns possessed only eight basic items: a robe, a bowl, a belt, a razor, a needle, a filter for drinking water, a walking stick and a toothpick. Nowadays they may also own such other important items as an umbrella or heavy jacket.

A monk shaves another monk's head. A shaved head is a sign of humility.

The eight-spoked wheel is called the Wheel of Dharma. It represents Buddhism's Eightfold Path, a way of life that helps people conquer their attachment to worldly things.

SACRED PAINTINGS

Like people of other religious faiths, Buddhists use art to express their beliefs. In Tibet and Bhutan, a country south of Tibet, professional artists paint thangkas (sacred paintings) on silk. These artists, whose work forms part of their religious devotion, are greatly respected in their communities. The thangka is used for meditation. Subjects for these works include Buddha and stories from saints' lives. The pictures vary in size from very small to huge. A large thangka can take a team of artists several months to create. In Bhutan, thangkas also may feature cliffs, woods, mountains and rivers. These elements of the landscape are considered special beings with a living soul, a belief that dates back to pre-Buddhist times.

A man paints an image of the Buddha by a roadside in Bhutan.

A seal appears on foods certified as kosher. Observant Jews follow rules about the kinds of foods they may eat and how they should be prepared.

The Middle East

Jewish Customs

Devout Jews follow various daily rituals as a way of remembering God in all they do. The day starts and ends with prayer. Special clothes are part of the ritual of prayer. Food must be prepared in particular ways to make sure it is kosher (clean according to Jewish law), and some foods must be avoided. The Sabbath is the Jewish day of rest and has its own rituals. It is a day to be with family, to rest and to pray to God.

Incense burners are used in some Jewish homes on the Sabbath. The fragrant rising smoke symbolises prayers carried up to God.

A protective case for the mezuzah scroll.

At Home

A mezuzah is a small scroll of parchment (a writing material made from animal skin) on which is written the beginning of the most important Jewish prayer, called the Shema: "Hear, O Israel: The Lord our God, the Lord is one". The mezuzah is placed in a small case, which is attached to the right-hand side of nearly every doorpost in many Jewish homes. Mezuzahs are not attached to the doorposts of a bathroom because this room is not considered suitable for holy objects. Jews touch their fingers to their lips and then to the mezuzah on the front door when they enter or leave their home. In Israel, a mezuzah is fastened to the doorpost of all government offices.

Religious Devotion

Orthodox Jews, Jews who follow a strict interpretation of Jewish laws, pray three times a day—in the morning, afternoon and evening. They pray at home or in the synagogue. Orthodox men drape a prayer shawl around their shoulders. For morning prayers, they also wear tefillin, black boxes with leather straps that hold verses of scripture. Jewish men wear a yarmulka (also called a skullcap) on their head when they pray. In addition to offering formal prayers, Jewish people may offer personal prayers to God at any time.

This man prays at the Western Wall, also called the Wailing Wall, in Jerusalem. It is a holy site for Jews, and many people come from all over the world to pray there.

A poster written in Hebrew urges, "For your own sake, and the sake of your children, learn Hebrew"! Hebrew, the language of ancient Israel and the Hebrew Bible, was revived in the 1800s. Today it is the official language of the state of Israel.

THE MIDDLE EAST

The Middle East covers parts of northern Africa, southwestern Asia and southeastern Europe. Scholars disagree on which countries make up the Middle East. But many say the region consists of Bahrain, Cyprus, Egypt, Iran, Iraq, Israel, Jordan, Kuwait, Lebanon, Oman, Qatar, Saudi Arabia, Sudan, Syria, Turkey, United Arab Emirates and Yemen. The region is also the birthplace of three major religions—Judaism, Christianity and Islam.

Food Preparation

Orthodox Jews carefully follow a set of dietary rules called kashrut. All the food they eat must be kosher—that is, clean, and fit to eat according to Jewish law. Only certain kinds of meat, such as chicken, beef and lamb, may be eaten. The animals must be slaughtered in a special way to cause minimum pain. Meat and dairy products must never be served at the same meal. For example, if people are eating meat, they may not have butter on their bread. Traditional Jewish families use one set of dishes for meat and another for milk products.

Hasidic Jews wear fur hats with a yarmulka underneath. They also wear peyot (side curls) on each side of the head.

Jewish men butcher fowl and oxen according to Jewish law, in an illustration from the 1400s. Kosher meat must be drained of blood.

Dress and Hygiene

Orthodox Jewish men always cover their heads to show respect to God. A cap called a yarmulka symbolises the superiority of God over the human mind. Orthodox men wear a prayer shawl called a tallit katan under their clothes. It is rectangular and has a hole for the head. Tassels on the four corners hang outside the clothes. They represent the four directions and show that God is everywhere. Jewish men who follow a form of Judaism called Hasidism grow their beards long and wear hats and dark clothes. Hasidic women cover their heads with a scarf or wig and always dress modestly.

A Jewish butcher prepares meat. Orthodox Jews always buy their meat from a kosher butcher shop.

THE SABBATH

Shabbat— the Sabbath—is a holy day of rest and worship for orthodox Jews. All food is prepared beforehand, and most forms of work are forbidden. Shabbat begins at sunset Friday and lasts until sunset Saturday. The mother begins the holy day by lighting and blessing the Shabbat candles. The family may go to synagogue and then gather for a special meal. The meal begins with blessings over the challah (the Shabbat bread) and wine. It is the best meal of the week and is long and leisurely. On Saturday morning, Jews may go to synagogue, where the rabbi leads prayers and gives a sermon. Afterwards, they spend a quiet afternoon reading scripture, telling stories and relaxing. At the end of Shabbat, Jews perform the havdalah ceremony, which separates Shabbat from the rest of the week. Blessings are said over wine, spices and a candle.

A mother lights the Sabbath candles as her daughter learns the ritual.

Rituals in Muslim Countries

Certain traditions are common to all Muslim countries, though customs vary to some degree. Practising Muslims follow the rituals detailed in the *Qur'an*, their sacred book. They pray five times a day to Allah (God) wherever they are. Both men and women dress modestly. Muslims use various greetings drawn from the *Qur'an* when they meet. They are known for their gracious hospitality. Guests are always welcomed with coffee and often a meal. Sufi Muslims have their own rituals, the most well known of which is a spinning dance. They believe the movements help the dancer come closer to Allah.

Coffee beans represent Muslim hospitality and fellowship. In many Muslim countries, men visit coffee houses for discussions and to exchange gossip.

A special container is used for storing the Qur'an at home. The holy book is treated with great respect.

Religious Devotion

Before prayers, Muslims usually prepare themselves with wudu (ritual washing). It is a purification ritual during which different parts of the body are washed in a particular order—hands, head, arms to elbows, feet—with clean running water. Muslims then face the direction of the holiest city of Islam, Mecca, Saudi Arabia, to pray. The *Qur'an* also contains laws regarding food. Devout Muslims never eat pork. Animals killed for food must be slaughtered swiftly and painlessly, and all the blood must be drained.

Muslims are taught to wash in a certain way before they enter a mosque to pray.

Two boys hug in greeting. Children are taught to greet others in the same way that adults do.

Etiquette, Greetings and Forms of Address

When two Muslims meet, they may exchange an Islamic greeting in which the first person says, "As-Salamu-Alaykum" ("Peace be with you"), and the other person replies, "Wa-Alaykum-as-Salam" ("And on you be peace"). Two men may shake hands and then each brings his hand back to his own heart. They also may hug and kiss each other when they meet. Muslim men and women who are not related are forbidden to touch each other, so they do not shake hands or embrace when meeting.

Dress and Hygiene

Muslims believe clothes should always be freshly washed and kept clean. Both men and women dress modestly. The extent to which women cover their bodies varies depending on where they live. In some places, they wear Western dress with a headscarf. In others, they cover their clothes with a long, dark dress when they leave home. In some countries, women wear a tentlike garment called a burqa (also spelled burka).

This antique coffee pot is from Turkey.

Guests and Hospitality

The *Qur'an* teaches Muslims to be hospitable to visitors. Fresh coffee served in little cups is the essential sign of welcome. It is made with sugar and sometimes cardamom, a deliciously scented spice. In Muslim countries, people often serve dishes made with meat and rice.

A Muslim family in Tehran, Iran, displays typical modest dress. Tradition requires a woman to cover her hair and neck. Some women cover their faces as well.

Whirling dervishes perform a famous Sufi ritual. The dance has important religious significance.

THE SUFIS

Sufism is a school of thought within Islam. Sufis differ from other Muslims in their desire to create a closer personal relationship with Allah. Dervishes are Sufi mystics who practise exercises called dhikrs. One of these is the whirling dance practised by Turkish Sufis. The Sufis spin around and around, losing themselves in the movements and becoming absorbed in Allah.

A chalice is used to hold wine during the celebration of Mass. Catholics believe the priest changes the wine into the blood of Jesus Christ.

Europe and the Americas

Rituals and Beliefs

A priest elevates (holds up) a chalice during Mass. Wine and wafers (small pieces of bread) are distributed to the congregation.

Many European rituals are linked to Christianity, the chief religion of the continent. The Mass or Eucharist is an important daily or weekly ritual for millions. Certain beliefs and superstitions, such as not walking under ladders, date back to early Christian times. It was considered bad luck to walk through a triangle, such as the one made by a leaning ladder, because a triangle symbolises the Trinity (God as the Father; the Son, Christ; and the Holy Spirit). Other rituals have non-religious origins. The sauna has its origins in the cleansing and healing rituals of Finland. Many rituals and beliefs of European origin today are part of everyday life in the Americas because of European immigration to the Americas.

Religious Devotion

Daily prayer is often part of Christian life. Worshipping together is also important, and Christians meet to pray in church on Saturday evenings or Sundays. The service varies according to the church. The Mass or Eucharist is celebrated to remember Jesus's Last Supper with his disciples. In Catholic churches, the priest transforms the bread (wafer) and wine into the body and blood of Jesus Christ. The people then receive Christ Himself in Holy Communion. Church services usually include a sermon, Bible reading, prayers and singing. Some churches use music and drama to increase the beauty and significance of their services. Other Christians prefer to worship more quietly or even in silence.

A Christian girl says prayers before bedtime as part of her daily routine.

CHURCH BELLS

The tradition of bell-ringing dates back to the Middle Ages, in the days before people had clocks. Church bells were rung at important times of the day, both for religious and non-religious reasons, such as announcing curfew. Church bells are still rung in many countries in Europe and the Americas. In the Russian Orthodox Church, for example, the ringing of bells calls the faithful to come for services and announces the beginning of various parts of the service to those who are not able to attend. One large bell is rung to call the congregation to worship. Church bells are rung in a solemn fashion at funerals when the body is taken from the church for burial. The bells are rung in turn, from the smallest to the largest. This symbolises the stages of the person's life on Earth, from infancy through adulthood, old age and death.

The bell tower of the cathedral in Florence, Italy.

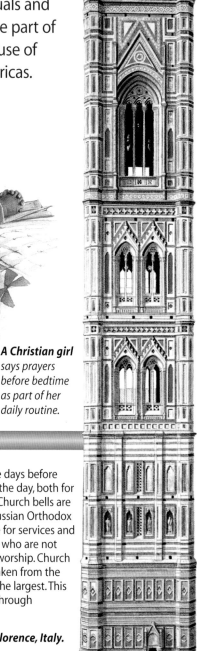

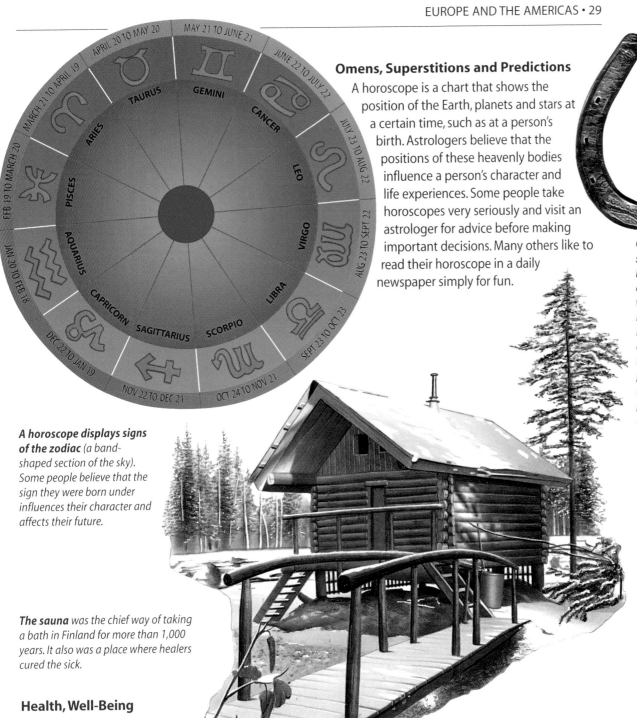

A horoscope displays signs of the zodiac (a band-shaped section of the sky). Some people believe that the sign they were born under influences their character and affects their future.

Omens, Superstitions and Predictions

A horoscope is a chart that shows the position of the Earth, planets and stars at a certain time, such as at a person's birth. Astrologers believe that the positions of these heavenly bodies influence a person's character and life experiences. Some people take horoscopes very seriously and visit an astrologer for advice before making important decisions. Many others like to read their horoscope in a daily newspaper simply for fun.

One superstition says that a horseshoe hung above a doorway will bring good luck. In most of Europe, it is hung with the open end pointing down. In the United States and parts of Ireland and Britain, the open end points up so the luck does not run out.

GOD BLESS YOU. During a worldwide epidemic in the A.D. mid-500s, sneezing violently was identified as a symptom of the disease, probably plague, that killed millions. The pope advised people to bless those who sneezed because they would die shortly.

The sauna was the chief way of taking a bath in Finland for more than 1,000 years. It also was a place where healers cured the sick.

Health, Well-Being and Survival

Since the time of the ancient Romans, people have visited spas to treat their ailments. Spas are towns situated on the site of a natural spring or well, whose waters are believed to have healing properties. Traditionally, a Finnish sauna was a hut by a lake, where stones were heated by burning wood. When the stones were baking hot, bathers threw cold water on them, creating steam. After basking in the steam, they dived into the cold lake. This was believed to improve blood circulation. Nowadays, many modern Finnish houses have an electric sauna in the bathroom. Saunas are also found in health clubs and homes in many other countries.

The Gellert Thermal Baths in Budapest, Hungary, is among the world's most famous spas.

Friends and Food

Europeans spend much of their free time meeting with friends. Many social gatherings, such as dinner parties, take place in the home. These are usually informal occasions for friends to just chat and spend time together. Bars and cafés are also common meeting places throughout Europe. In England, the pub is a popular place for socialising. In recent years, many English pubs have become more like bars in continental Europe, which serve food and hot drinks as well as beer and soft drinks. The tradition of afternoon tea is still strong in England, although younger people are increasingly turning to the continental favourite—coffee.

Meeting and chatting with friends over a cup of coffee is part of European social life.

Spanish women greet each other by kissing each other on both cheeks. A man meeting a woman will do the same, but men usually shake hands.

IN GREECE, guests are usually welcomed with preserves, water and coffee. It is considered bad manners to refuse. According to custom, they first drink the water, then eat the preserves. The coffee is enjoyed last.

Etiquette, Greetings and Forms of Address

In the northern countries of Germany, Sweden and the Netherlands, people tend to be more formal when meeting, and shaking hands is common. In the southern countries of Spain, Italy and Greece, greetings are warmer and often include hugs and kisses. However, in business or when addressing older people, it is still common to use formal titles and last names. In Spain, men are addressed as señor; young women as señorita; and married women as señora. In more traditional areas, the titles don for a man and doña for a woman are used with the first name to show respect.

People enjoy a drink outside an English pub.
Beer is the favourite drink, though wine has become popular and soft drinks are also served.

TIME WITH FRIENDS

The word pub is short for public house. The first pubs in England were the tabernae (taverns), introduced by the Romans almost 2,000 years ago. Food and wine and probably the local ale (a sweet, strong alcohol) were served there. After the Romans left Britain, the tabernae disappeared. Over the centuries, alehouses replaced them. During the Middle Ages, water supplies were often polluted, and ale was considered a safer drink—even for children. In the United Kingdom today, the pub is still a popular place to meet friends or socialise with workmates. People also hold celebrations at pubs. In many villages and towns, the pub is the heart of the community. Nowadays, many pubs welcome families and offer good food. Pub games such as darts and billiards are also a popular tradition.

People enjoy a traditional afternoon tea in which scones (thick, flat cakes) with jam and cream are served. Having tea at a tea shop is popular, especially among older people.

Food Preparation and Mealtimes

Tea was introduced into England in the 1600s. People of that time believed that it had healing properties. The first tea shop opened in London in 1717, but only the wealthy drank there because tea was very expensive. In the late 1700s, as more tea was shipped to England, the price fell and more people could afford to drink it. The tradition of taking afternoon tea developed as a social event with strict rules. A proper teapot, cups, saucers, tea strainers, teaspoons and sugar bowls were essential. In the late 1800s and early 1900s, it was acceptable to pour hot tea into a saucer to cool it before drinking it.

A tea set from the Edwardian times of the early 1900s consists of a teapot, left, hot-water jug, middle, and milk jug.

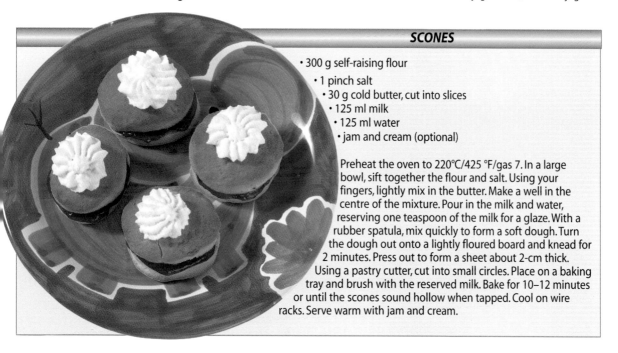

SCONES

- 300 g self-raising flour
- 1 pinch salt
- 30 g cold butter, cut into slices
- 125 ml milk
- 125 ml water
- jam and cream (optional)

Preheat the oven to 220°C/425 °F/gas 7. In a large bowl, sift together the flour and salt. Using your fingers, lightly mix in the butter. Make a well in the centre of the mixture. Pour in the milk and water, reserving one teaspoon of the milk for a glaze. With a rubber spatula, mix quickly to form a soft dough. Turn the dough out onto a lightly floured board and knead for 2 minutes. Press out to form a sheet about 2-cm thick. Using a pastry cutter, cut into small circles. Place on a baking tray and brush with the reserved milk. Bake for 10–12 minutes or until the scones sound hollow when tapped. Cool on wire racks. Serve warm with jam and cream.

TEA-TIME ETIQUETTE
- Sugar should be served only in cubes.
- Loose-leaf tea should be used in place of tea bags.
- It is rude to clink the side of your cup while stirring. Once finished stirring, gently place your spoon on the saucer behind the cup without making any noise.
- Scones should be spread first with jam and a bit of cream.
- Hold a teacup with the index finger through the handle and the thumb just above. The middle finger secures the grip. The last two fingers should never be used.

American Traditions

The peoples of the USA and Canada have much in common. They share their history of building a North American society with its roots in Europe. Yet there are certain differences. Americans from the USA are often seen as outgoing and friendly, and more willing to take risks in life. In general, Canadians tend to take life at a slower pace and are more cautious. Americans are known for their patriotism while Canadians are less likely to revel in national glory. English is the national language in the USA, while Canada is a dual-language nation with both English and French-speaking regions.

Coffee is imported to North America from such countries as Brazil, Vietnam and Colombia.

JAMAICA BLUE

KONA

For some Americans, meals are often eaten on the go. *Fast-food restaurants are popular. Hamburgers, hot dogs and French fries satisfy the appetites of many hungry Americans.*

CANADA IS THE WORLD'S SECOND LARGEST COUNTRY IN AREA, including land and inland water. It occupies a total of 9,970,610 square km (6,195,737 square miles), but only one-tenth of the land area is inhabited. Much of the land north of Canada's forests is barren, made up of icefields and tundra.

The red maple leaf is Canada's symbol *and appears on the nation's flag. Canada is the world's greatest producer of maple syrup.*

THE AMERICAS

The continents of North America and South America make up the Western Hemisphere. North America contains Canada, Greenland, the United States, Mexico, Central America and the Caribbean Sea islands. South America contains Argentina, Bolivia, Brazil (which occupies almost half the continent), Chile, Colombia, Ecuador, Guyana, Paraguay, Peru, Suriname, Uruguay and Venezuela.

Two boys greet each other with a "high-five". *They slap their palms together while holding their forearms raised.*

Food Preparation and Mealtimes

Because North America is home to people from around the world, Canadians and Americans enjoy a huge variety of foods. Maple syrup made from the sap of maple trees and used by the native people before the arrival of European settlers, is just one original American treat. Mexican burritos and salsa are as common as hamburgers and fries. Americans love their coffee, and the United States is the largest consumer of coffee beans in the world. Every morning and afternoon, millions of people stop for a few minutes to enjoy a cup of coffee. Americans drink about 400 million cups of coffee each day!

Etiquette, Greetings and Forms of Address

When people in the United States and Canada meet for the first time, they usually shake hands. Male friends shake hands when they meet or they may embrace. Female friends may exchange a kiss on the cheek. The "high-five" features two peoples' hands slapping at face level or above. Originally a greeting used by sports players in the United States to congratulate teammates who scored in a match, the high-five is now used around the world as a joyful greeting or a sign of victory.

AT THE START OF THE SCHOOL DAY

Because the United States is a nation of people from many different countries and cultures, it is considered important to build loyalty and national pride. At the start of every school day, many schoolchildren stand in front of a U.S. flag and recite the Pledge of Allegiance to their country. The pledge is believed to have been written by Francis Bellamy (1855–1931), an American clergyman and editor. It was first recited in 1892 as part of the celebrations for the 400th anniversary of Christopher Columbus's landing in America. The pledge has been slightly changed since then and today is said as follows: "I pledge allegiance to the Flag of the United States of America and to the Republic for which it stands, one Nation under God, indivisible with liberty and justice for all".

American schoolchildren, hand on heart, face the U.S. flag and recite the Pledge of Allegiance.

Health, Well-Being and Survival

With the popularity of fast and convenient food, the American diet has become high in sugary and fatty foods. As a result, large numbers of Americans are obese. In recent years, however, more Americans have turned to low-fat foods. Many also take exercise seriously, jogging in the park, exercising at home or going to a gym. Many Americans and Canadians are members of sports clubs or teams, which make staying healthy and fit fun.

A baseball player hits a ball. Baseball is one of North America's favourite sports.

Cycling is a popular North American sport. Special events such as bike rallies and races to raise money for charity encourage this healthy habit.

Watching TV is a favourite American pastime.

Ice hockey is the most popular sport in Canada. The first game was played in Canada in the late 1800s. The long Canadian winters provide many icy fields and lakes for hockey lovers.

At Home

In many American homes, entertainment centres on the TV. Gathering together to watch a special programme or sports event is a common family activity.

The headdress is the most recognisable item of American Indian clothing. It was a symbol of high status or bravery.

A young American Indian from Cody, Wyoming, wears traditional clothing at a powwow.

BEFORE AMERICAN INDIANS ACQUIRED HORSES IN THE 1700s, they moved on foot, often disguised in wolf skins so they would not frighten away the buffalo.

American Indians hunted buffalo during the summer, killing just enough to provide for their needs.

American Indians

Many groups of people lived in what is now Canada and the United States before European explorers and settlers arrived. The groups had different cultures and daily practices. For example, the people of the Great Plains in northern North America depended on buffalo for food, clothing and tools. They also used the skins to build shelters called tepees. Each Indian nation had distinctive clothing, which is sometimes worn today for ceremonies. American Indians relied on herbal medicines and conducted healing ceremonies to treat people who were ill.

A headdress made from buffalo skin is decorated with horns. The people of the Great Plains held special religious ceremonies before a hunt to ensure their success.

Dress and Hygiene

The Plains Indians used buffalo skin to make clothing. They decorated beautiful robes with bright patterns. American Indians wore elaborate jewellery and headdresses, also called war bonnets. War bonnets made of fur, feathers and buffalo horn were worn on special occasions. Each feather represented a brave deed by a warrior. Hair grooming was also important, often symbolising one's status. Hopi women wore an elaborate hairdo called the squash-blossom hairdo upon reaching adulthood.

Food Preparation and Mealtimes

Plains Indians often hunted the buffalo on the open plain. Sometimes, they forced the animals over cliffs to their death. Some of the meat was roasted and eaten immediately. The rest was dried and stored for the winter.

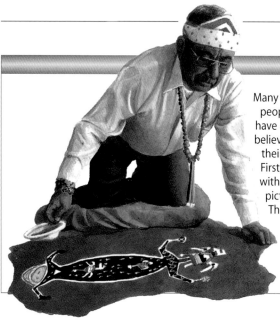

NAVAJO SAND PAINTINGS

Many American Indians used herbal medicines to treat people with disease. For hundreds of years, the Navajo have also constructed sand paintings, which they believe rid people of the evil magic that has caused their sickness. The designs are made on a bed of sand. First, the sand is smoothed down. The design is created with white, red, yellow, black and blue powder. Elaborate pictures may take many men and women a whole day to complete. The sick person then sits on the picture to absorb its powers, and the shaman (priest or medicine man) prays and chants. After the ceremony, the picture is destroyed.

A Navajo creates a sand painting.

The coloured sand used in sand painting is made from ground minerals and plants, such as sandstone, charcoal, pollen and flower petals.

Health, Well-Being and Survival

The sweat lodge is central to most American Indian cultures and spiritual life. The lodge usually has a dome-shaped frame made of saplings. It is covered by animal skins or canvas. Inside is a sacred fire pit, where stones are heated. Water is poured on the stones to create steam. A leader begins the prayers, songs and chants. Indians believe that sweating helps people to purify the body, cure illness and influence spirits. To aid the process of purification, people may fast for a day before entering a sweat lodge. According to another Native American tradition, dream catchers trap bad dreams and let good dreams float down to sleepers.

The entrance to a sweat lodge often faces east, the direction of the rising sun. This represents a new spiritual beginning.

DREAM CATCHERS

- thin bendable branches
- coloured string
- coloured beads
- feathers

Tie one or two branches together to make a hoop. Tie a piece of string to the hoop and string some

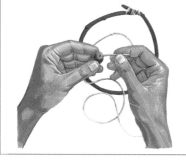

beads along it. Tie the end of this string to the opposite side of the hoop. Repeat this process as many times as necessary to form a colourful starlike pattern inside the hoop. Tie some pieces of string to the bottom part of the hoop. String some beads along them and

tie a feather to the end of each string. Finally, tie a piece of string to the top of your dream catcher and make a loop for hanging.

Latin America

Latin America embraces a vast array of cultures, including native people, descendants of European settlers and African slaves. Native cultures stress the relationship between people and the natural and spirit worlds. These are often reflected in art and weaving. Showing hospitality to guests is an honoured tradition throughout Latin America. In several countries, sharing maté (a drink made from the maté plant) is a daily ritual.

A Huichol woman from Mexico has painted her face for the peyote ceremony. During this ceremony the sacred peyote cactus plant is eaten. Most peyote ceremonies involve drumming, singing, praying and telling stories to offer thanks to the Creator for this blessing.

A cuia and bombilha used to serve maté tea. Drinking maté is an important ritual and it is rude to refuse an invitation to drink it.

Etiquette, Greetings and Forms of Address

In most Latin American countries, both men and women greet each other with a warm hug. Costa Rica is rather different. Greetings are more North American in style. Men offer a firm handshake, and women often greet each other with a handshake or light kiss. The correct form of address is important in Costa Rica. The title Don should be used before a man's first name—for example, Don José. Doña is used before a woman's name.

Touching knuckles is a gesture of greeting where the people reflect a mixture of African, American Indian and European roots.

Guests and Hospitality

Across much of Argentina, Uruguay, Paraguay and southern Brazil, groups of family, friends and co-workers enjoy the daily ritual of sharing maté. Maté is a drink made from the dried leaves and twigs of a South American holly. It is prepared in a hollowed-out gourd. The gourd is half-filled with maté and topped with hot water. After seven to ten minutes, the brew is sipped through a bombilla. A bombilla is a straw with a strainer at one end. The server takes the first sip, then offers the gourd to each guest. Each person drinks the whole amount of liquid in the gourd and then passes it back to the server for refilling with water.

A local shaman from the Matse people of Peru tends medicinal plants in the Amazon rain forest. Because many shamans are old and have no apprentices, their ancient art is dying out.

Health, Well-Being and Survival

To keep healthy in mind and body, the people of the Amazon rain forest rely on their shaman, who is a wise man and spiritual leader. His advice is sought by all. Shamans have a broad knowledge of forest plants, which they use to make remedies for a wide range of health problems. They also use magic to chase away evil spirits that are believed to cause suffering, and to ask the gods to cure the sick.

WEAVING

In Guatemala, weaving is a great source of pride. The bright colours and designs of the woven cloth reflect the traditions of the Maya, the country's native people. The designs include a wide variety of geometric patterns, animals and scenes from ancient myths. Almost all Mayan women own a loom, and many weave for their own needs. They use a horizontal loom, tied at one end to their waist. The other end is attached to a tree branch. Threads are made of cotton and fibre from vegetable and insect sources. Interestingly, the men crochet the morales, the bags often used to carry the midday meal Guatemalans take to work.

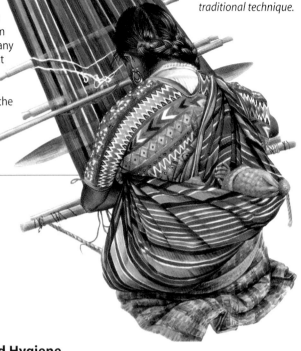

A Maya woman weaves on a handloom using a traditional technique.

THE BORORO INDIANS OF MATO GRASSO STATE IN BRAZIL believe that newly harvested maize should not be eaten until a shaman has blessed it. The shaman dances and sings, gradually rising to a higher spiritual state in which he performs the blessing. The Bororo believe that without this ceremony, their people would perish.

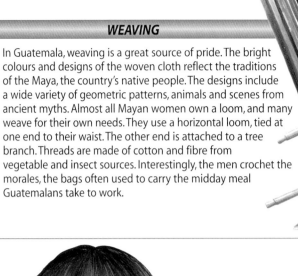

Dress and Hygiene

The people of the Amazon rain forest use distinctive ornaments to express their identity and to convey special meanings. The Matsé people who live in the western part of the Amazon rain forest worship the jaguar for its beauty and stealth. Many adults decorate the lower parts of their faces with blue tattoos and pierce their chins and noses with sticks so they resemble a jaguar.

A Huichol craftsman painting beaded animal sculptures. Although Huichol artwork is made for prayer offerings, some works are also made for interested art collectors.

Religious Devotion

The Huichol people of the states of Nayarit and Jalisco in Mexico have succeeded in maintaining their traditional culture, language and spiritual life for many centuries. Like other American Indians, they believe in a spirit world that they can communicate with through symbols and rituals. The Huichol express their religious feelings through artwork, such as yarn paintings and beaded sculpture. Designs of Huichol art work are inspired by visions or dreams of an individual artist. The special techniques, which involve the pressing of yarn or beads into wax, are passed down from generation to generation.

African Rituals

The people of Africa inhabit a vast continent with a wide variety of landscapes. Africa has hundreds of nations, groups and clans, each with its own history and culture. In some areas, religions such as Islam or Christianity have many followers, but in others, traditional beliefs are still the most important. Whatever religion the people follow, Africans perform rituals out of respect for their culture or ancestors. Many Africans believe that the spirit world and the human world are very close and can be connected through ritual.

Religious Devotion

Traditional Africans believe in a supreme god who created the world and everything in it. This god is, however, too important and remote to bother with daily events. He has appointed lesser gods or spirits to manage the natural world and human affairs. Some of these gods look after natural events, such as rain or wind, while others care for a particular place or group of people. Shrines are often built to the local gods, and a priest or priestess cares for the shrine. One of the priest's or priestess's most important duties is to feed the god by sprinkling food, drink or blood on the shrine. People ask for the god's help by making offerings or sacrifices through the priest or priestess.

A decorated calabash gourd is used in Cameroon to store the bones of ancestors. The bones are used in rituals.

Africa

Asie Usu, a nature spirit, is carved by the Baule people of West Africa.

AFRICA

Africa lies south of Europe and west of Asia and contains 53 independent countries. Tropical rain forests dominate western and central Africa. The world's largest desert, the Sahara, stretches across northern Africa. Africa also has the world's longest river—the Nile. Much of the continent is grassland. In the north, most of the people are Arabs. The great majority of the African population lives south of the Sahara.

THE TOGU NA

In many African cultures, people erect special buildings for religious or ceremonial purposes. The Dogon people of Mali build a togu na, a rectangular house with a flat roof supported by large wooden posts. The men of the village meet in the togu na to discuss problems or disputes and to make communal decisions, such as when to plant the crops. Although women are not allowed to enter the togu na, the posts are often carved with pictures of women. The Dogon also build binu, shrines dedicated to mythical clan ancestors. These may be an animal or a spirit. Another important Dogon building is the ginna, a house built near the village, often on a hill from which the village can be clearly seen. The ginna is the home of the oldest man in the village, who looks after the statues of the gods and other sacred objects.

The upright posts supporting the roof of a togu na are often carved with symbols and sacred signs.

Health, Well-Being and Survival

In many African villages, one person holds spiritual powers. This person is believed to be in very close communication with the gods and spirits. This person is able to decide the will of the gods in disputes between neighbours and can bring the god's power to help a sick person. The Yoruba people of West Africa believe the power of the spirits and gods can be harnessed by the performance of the Egungun Mask Dance. Between June and November, depending on where they live, Yoruba men dance through villages wearing masks and costumes that represent different gods. It is believed that the gods enter the dancers. If the dancer stumbles or touches a person, it is the god's way of giving bad or good luck.

An Egungun dancer *moves through a village in Benin.*

A wand used during the Ifa prediction ceremony *is carved in the shape of a woman with sacred headgear.*

Omens, Superstitions and Predictions

Among the Yoruba, who live in Nigeria and Benin, the Ifa ceremony is a widespread method of prediction. A person wishing to know the future asks a question of a priest. The priest spreads sawdust on a sacred tray and drops 16 palmnuts. The resulting pattern refers to a sacred verse. The priest recites the verse from memory, and the person wishing to know the future looks for clues in the story for the answer to his or her question.

A priest of the Yoruba people *prepares for an Ifa ceremony in which he will predict the future.*

This amulet *(magic charm) from West Africa is made of shells and teeth. It was used to cast healing spells on sick people.*

Daily Life in Africa

The people of Africa have developed a wide range of lifestyles influenced by climates of the regions where they live and how they grow their food. In the south and east, vast open plains of grass provide fodder for large herds of cattle and good growing conditions for millet and grain. In central and western Africa, where the climate is damp and hot, farmers raise such crops as yam, rice or okra. In some areas, people live in small villages, but many Africans live in cities.

Images of ancestors adorn a pendant from Burkina Faso in western Africa. Such pendants are worn to obtain protection and blessings from ancestors.

Dress and Hygiene

Body decorations, clothing and ornaments were once dictated by social structure and carried deep symbolic meaning across Africa. For example, in Zaire, eagle feathers could be worn only by chiefs. However, customs have changed in recent decades, and now many adults wear eagle feathers. Today in many westernised African countries, body ornaments are worn to symbolise tradition and identity and are worn on special occasions. Because the climate across much of Africa is relatively warm, clothing is rarely thick or heavy. In some areas people wear a cloth around their waists and decorative beads or jewellery. In most areas, Western-style shirts and trousers are worn.

A woman from Mali displays wealth in the form of an elaborate headdress made of silver, copper, amber and glass beads.

At Home

Traditional African homes vary enormously in size, shape and style. They are usually made from local materials, such as wood, thatch or stone. Dried mud is also a widespread building material. For these houses, the earth is mixed with water, moulded into shape, then allowed to dry rock hard in the sun. The roof of the structure is made of thatch (dried grass). Peoples of southern Africa often paint the outside of their houses with bright colours and bold designs. In Sudan, people insert objects, such as plates or tin cans, in the mud walls as they dry for decoration.

Bright colours and designs decorate this Ndebele house in South Africa.

AFRICAN MODERNIZATION

The withdrawal of the European colonial powers during the 1800s and 1900s was followed by political unrest and chaos in many African countries. Today much of Africa is still affected by war, hunger, disease and poverty. Corrupt governments, civil wars and weak economies have worsened living conditions of the growing African population. Droughts, floods and other natural disasters have also caused famine. One of the biggest health problems today is AIDS. Today, many local governments and international organisations are helping Africans to live healthier lives and fight poverty. In recent years, many new schools have been founded to provide children in poor communities with an education.

Schoolchildren in Durban, South Africa, practise their lessons.

ABISH FROM ETHIOPIA

- 60 ml vegetable oil
- 1 onion, chopped
- 1 tablespoon grated ginger
- 1 tablespoon garlic, finely chopped
- 2 tomatoes, chopped
- 500 g minced beef
- 1 teaspoon salt
- 1 tablespoon butter, melted
- 1 tablespoon chopped parsley
- 1 tablespoon turmeric
- 250 g goat's cheese (optional)
- parsley, to garnish

Warm the oil in a large frying pan over low heat. Add the onion and cook until opaque, stirring occasionally. Mix in the ginger, garlic, tomatoes, beef and salt. Cook for 15–20 minutes, stirring often, until the meat is cooked. Arrange on a serving plate. In a small bowl, mix 1 tablespoon of parsley with the butter. Add turmeric to the butter mixture and spoon over the meat. Top with goat's cheese and sprinkle with parsley. Serve with rice or freshly-made bread.

An Ethiopian woman makes injera, large, flat bread that accompanies most meals in that country.

Food Preparation and Mealtime

Each region of Africa has its own type of food and way of preparing it. In West Africa, the basis of most meals is either rice or fufu, the pounded roots of yam or cassava. A large dish of rice or fufu is placed in the centre of the table, surrounded by smaller dishes of stewed meat or vegetables. Each diner takes a small handful of rice or fufu, mixes it with meat or vegetables and rolls it into a ball. In East Africa, millet is more common. This grain is ground into flour and then baked or fried into large flat breads. Diners tear the bread into pieces and then use the bread pieces to scoop up meat or vegetables.

An East African family gathers around a communal food bowl.

Guests and Hospitality

Most traditional African foods are eaten with the fingers of one hand without knives, forks or even spoons. In many areas, people use the right hand for eating, greeting guests or any other activity that involves other people. The left hand is used for personal hygiene. Guests are often provided with a small dish of water in which to wash their right hands before and after a meal. Highly respected guests may have water poured over their hands by their hostess.

This small kava bowl is from the Fijian Islands, where kava is a drink used in rituals.

A large bowl of kava, a fermented drink made from the kava roots, is stirred by a Polynesian householder as he prepares to serve it to his guests.

Australasia and the Pacific

Although the people of Australasia and Oceania may be separated by vast stretches of the Pacific Ocean, they share many customs and beliefs. The sea is a major influence on their cultures and lifestyles. Some scientists divide the people of Oceania into three main ethnic and cultural groups: Melanesian, Micronesian and Polynesian. Whatever their group, most people in the Pacific Islands live in small farming or fishing villages. They often follow the same customs as their ancestors did.

Australasia and Oceania

AUSTRALASIA AND OCEANIA

Australasia and Oceania lie east of Asia and west of the Americas. Australasia refers to the continent of Australia, plus New Guinea, New Zealand, and other nearby islands. New Guinea and New Zealand are also considered as part of the Pacific Islands, or Oceania. Oceania is a name given to a group of many thousands of islands scattered across the Pacific Ocean. New Guinea is the largest island in the group. It contains Papua, which is a part of Indonesia, and the independent country of Papua New Guinea. Islands near the mainland of Asia (Indonesia, Japan, the Philippines) are part of Asia. Islands near North and South America (the Aleutians, the Galapagos) are grouped with those continents.

Guests and Hospitality

Polynesians have traditionally extended a warm, lavish welcome to visitors. In each village, there is a house called the marai where visitors may stay free of charge. When strangers arrive, they are first challenged to see if they are peaceful. If they are, they are welcomed by touching noses. Once in the marai, visitors are served a special drink called kava as music is played. Only after this formal welcome do the Polynesians ask why a visitor has arrived and what his or her business might be.

A Maori man from New Zealand challenges a visitor with wide eyes and a protruding tongue to declare if he or she comes in peace.

MAKE A POLYNESIAN LEI

and around your neck, like a necklace. Then fasten the last link through the first to complete the chain. Add coloured flower-shaped pieces of paper to the chain, stapling or taping one flower to each link. Wear your lei to dinner or a celebration.

- a sheet of green paper cut into strips approximately 2.5 cm (1 inch) wide and13 cm (5 inches) long
- a sheet of white paper cut into flower shapes
- a sheet of yellow paper cut into flower shapes

- a stapler or tape

Loop one of the strips of green paper to form a link and staple or tape the ends securely. Loop a second strip of green paper through the first and staple or tape the ends. You should have two chain links. Continue to add to the chain of green paper links until the chain is long enough to fit over your head

Health, Well-Being and Survival

In Polynesia and Melanesia, wooden carvings of gods and spirits are used to help ensure success and survival. Some clans in Melanesia have a sacred wooden board that is kept hidden. It is believed that as long as the board is kept safe, the clan will survive wars and famines. In Polynesia, wooden carvings of the gods are placed over doorways to ensure that the person who lives there benefits from the protection of the god portrayed. Temples are adorned with magnificent wooden carvings of the gods and their spirits, which are believed to ensure the god will visit the area. Polynesians also create beautiful garlands called leis to give to one another or to dedicate to the gods on special occasions. Leis may be made from shells, leaves or feathers, but the most popular are made from flowers. In the islands of Micronesia, wooden masks are painted to resemble the gods. Men wear these masks during dances to attract the favour of the gods.

A board carved with the figure of an ancestor is kept hidden by some clans in Melanesia.

A tiki is a Maori neck pendant in the form of a human figure. The word tiki means human image, but it is also the name of carved figures of the gods.

THE HULA

The famous hula dance of Hawaii began as a religious ceremony. While a priest chanted the story of a god or goddess to the beat of a drum, the dancer moved in time to the beat, using hands and body movements to describe the story being told. Later the dance was adapted for stories about heroes or kings as well. Christian missionaries working in Hawaii attempted to ban the hula dance because of its links to the old religion. Although King Kalakaua was Christian, he revived the hula in the 1870s and insisted that the words and movements be recorded. Recent years have seen the development of a form of modern hula that links the traditional dance and movements to modern songs and rhythms. It is now a popular part of Hawaiian culture that is taught to schoolchildren throughout the islands.

A Hawaiian dances the hula to the beat of a traditional drum.

Glossary

Altar A table or raised platform on which offerings are placed, usually found in a church, temple or other place of worship.

Ancestor A family member from a preceding generation to whom you are directly related, for example, a grandfather or great-grandfather.

Astrologer A person who claims to know and interpret the supposed influence of the stars and planets on people or future events.

Blessing Divine favour or protection. An approval or wish for happiness.

Burial The act or ceremony of placing a dead body in a grave or tomb.

Burqa A long robe, from the top of the head to the ground, worn by some Muslim women.

Ceremony The celebration of an important event with an act or series of acts that follow a set of instructions established by a religion, culture or country.

Chant To sing in one tone or to repeat a prayer many times. A song or hymn used in religious ritual.

Convent A place where a community of religious people, such as nuns, live.

Culture A way of life. Every human society has a culture that includes its arts, beliefs, customs, institutions, inventions, language, technology and values.

Deity A god or goddess.

Devotion Earnestness in religion; religious worship or observance; act of devoting to a sacred use or purpose.

Devout Having strong religious beliefs.

Divine Sacred, being related to a god or goddess.

Drought A shortage of water for a long time.

Enlightenment The act of receiving spiritual or intellectual insight or information.

Equality The condition of being equal and treated as equal.

Etiquette Formal rules of behaviour in polite society.

Famine Shortage of food for a long time.

Funeral A religious or other ceremony that usually takes place before a dead body is buried or cremated (burned to ashes).

Generation People born within the same period of time.

Horoscope A diagram showing the position of the moon, sun and planets at a specific time, such as when someone was born. A horoscope is said to predict events in someone's life.

Hospitality Friendly and generous treatment of a guest or visitor.

Hygiene The maintenance of health and cleanliness in an individual person and within a group.

Incense A material that produces perfumed smoke when burned, usually made from plant products.

Indigenous people The original people living in a country or area before other people settled there, and their descendants.

Jews Descendants of an ancient people called the Hebrews or Israelites who practise Judaism.

Livestock Animals, such as cows and sheep, kept and raised for their produce.

Meditate To think privately or to focus one's mind on serious or religious thoughts.

Minority A group of people with their own identity who are outnumbered by larger groups.

Monastery A place where a community of religious people, such as monks, live.

Monk A man who has separated himself from ordinary ways of life to devote himself to his religion.

Mosque A place of worship and prayer for the followers of Islam.

Muslim A person who follows the religion of Islam.

Nomad A person who moves from place to place to find food for himself or herself or his or her livestock.

Nun A woman who has separated herself from ordinary ways of life to devote herself to her religion.

Omen A message or event believed to be a sign of what will happen in the future.

Purification The act of cleansing a person or object, often through ceremony or ritual.

Ritual A set of repeated actions done in a precise way, usually with a solemn meaning or significance.

Sacred Holy or precious.

Sacrifice The killing of an animal, which is offered to a god or gods as part of worship.

Saint A holy person who becomes a recognised religious hero by displaying a virtue or virtues valued by his or her religion. A patron saint is a holy person believed to protect the interests of a country, place, group, trade, profession or activity.

Sanctuary A sacred place or a place where sacred objects are stored.

Scripture Sacred, religious writing or a passage from the Bible.

Secular Worldly affairs, not religious or sacred.

Sermon A public religious speech made by a priest or minister.

Shaman A priest or doctor who uses magic to protect people and to cure the sick.

Shrine A small chapel, altar, or sacred place of worship.

Slaughter The killing of animals for food or ceremonial purposes.

Slave A person who is forced to work without pay. A slave is someone who is the property of another person and has no personal rights or freedom.

Spirit A good or bad supernatural being or force.

Supernatural Not of this world; beyond nature.

Superstition A belief or practice that is the result of an unreasonable fear. The belief that magic affects events.

Synagogue A Jewish house of worship and a centre of Jewish education and social life.

Torah The Hebrew name for the first five books of the Bible.

Tradition The beliefs, opinions, customs and stories passed from generation to generation by word of mouth or by practice.

Vegetarian A person who eats only plant-based foods and does not eat meat, fish, or some other animal products.

Vow A solemn promise made to another person or to God.

Zodiac An imaginary belt of the heavens divided into 12 constellations or equal parts.

Index